WOLFCRAFT

Wolfcraft

Poems

Narya Rose Deckard

BROKEN TRIBE PRESS

Wolfcraft is the 2024 Winner of the Tribe MFA Graduate Award

Front cover art by Matt Avery

Cover design by Jacob Arms
Published by Broken Tribe Press
Lawrence Landing Company
Raleigh, North Carolina 27609
USA, North America

Broken Tribe Press is a proud member of:

Independent Book Publishers Association
 and
Community of Literary Magazines and Presses

www.brokentribepress.com

BROKEN TRIBE PRESS

CONTENTS

Shapeshifters

Acknowledgements

Women Who Know Something More

"I beg you to believe it. Women that know something more do exist, night-women do exist, and what is up, they can make down." —Petronius Satyricon

By the wisdom of the rune ur!
By the screech owl's flight in the night!
We are women who know something more.

They slander us with shibboleths that drown our lore.
Our deaths they scribe with fear. They indict
Wisdom we gather from the rune ur.

They say locks can't hinder us: through the door's
Hinge we slip, your snatched children our appetite,
For they dread women who know something more.

But my potions of nettle, crabapple, and mugwort
Do not demand your child's blood, nor do I need
midnight pacts with the devil to find strength from the
wise rune ur,

Rather the metaphor I cast to wolves, chamomile, and
sycamores I beseech; for love, not power, is my
acolyte: As I commune, I know something more.

What we will from without, we implore
From within. Urðr, Norn of earth, delights
In our wisdom from the rune ur.
She blesses women who know something more.

Edge of Wolf

Donning Freya's Cloak of Feathers

My first move:
Stop buying those how-to guides,
texts that slap together rhymes
that invoke random deities
and call them spells. Learn to listen
to my intuition. Speak
my own poetry.

My second move:
Turn off, uninstall, and delete
social media apps where I've dithered
over posed photo shoots of #moonblessed crystals
deer skulls designer peasant dresses.
Magic can't be bought,
only given.

My third move:
Pick up my tools:
seeds, shovel, humus.
Don't you see the magic they do?
Work them into the earth.
Work my hands into the earth.
Get dirty every time.

My fourth move:
Wield my paper and pen.
Work my hands across the page
in thick ink furrows.
My fingers will be stained in the shape
of ancient runes carved in stone. They speak

wisdom. And those stains on my tongue?
They are the Mouth of the Wolf rising,
the moon waxing,
Freya's distaff shivering at dawn.

Wolf Fragments I

"In writing, beauty prefers an edge." - Anne Carson

I.

when i eat my alphabet
gardenbound in madder ink

empty my veins of blood
and flood them with ink

when the rising
moon dreamed dusk
spooned me
its shadows

wounds will be epithets for pain,
scars will be odes to the past

my ink a conduit
for silenced
voices

when moonfull
shadows exhale
my gloaming

I Am an Upside-Down Willow

I grow like a willow, in slow deepening circles.
A rabbit's bones lie splintered at my black roots,
her remains picked clean by soft dripping tongues and
hard black beaks. Follow her white cage, Follow her
pallid breath exhaled beneath my slender branches

To stones who speak in the slow tongue of bone.
To autumn when I shiver free what I no longer need.
Though sometimes I cling to a final brown leaf,
the reluctance of a young beech for change.

My stones crack and I bleed rich seams,
thick sticky red on moss;
White yarrow soaks up the remains.
Here comes death, cold,
the end of the stag god whose horned head rests on
snow while he sleeps.
We drink his blood, he who gave us the sun.

I ask myself: where do flowers go in winter?
Do we ever really die?
Or do we just fade from Earth's surface,
to be wintered Underground? The soil of ground
bone has true power.

The magic of rebirth and rebirth—
Daffodils and crocuses and lilies of the valley return
and return. But what lingers beyond death?
What death speaks to the living?
I speak myself unerased.

My body writes my story.
My body leads my way into the world,
to my dreams where I am the daffodil,
I am the willow upside down.
My roots reach through sky like flowers
who letter the Earth:

We are all on the edge of when dog meets wolf.
Death fathoms the soil's surface,
the edge of all being,
soil like my flesh.

Light Eaters

I let myself into the night
that inhales the ebbing light
like a whale who swallows
a mouthful of stars.
Oak snakes lick my ankles
with wolf-like tongues.
I've donned Freya's cloak of feathers,
my journey's end unknown
for I must follow
blindly with eyes
milk white or closed.
The beginning eats the end
until together they bend
like lunar light.
The wind's voice thickens;
a thousand voices of far-flung tongues

    silenced

by mouths of moon
flowers that drink the nectar
of stars and cut
sounds of light.
The bones at my feet
devour the blood
that drips from my dark.
My life feeds them;
chervil, bittercress, fennel
creep and twine
around ribs that sip

moonlight embered
in unmarrowed bones.
The hollow fills
where a heart once beat.
I circle
the thickening bones
like a wolf.
I wolf down fumitory,
plantain, and spells;
they coat my tongue,
the green and ancient pulp
bloom by her weaving,
wolf bleeds
   into my flesh,
   into a new darkness,
   into that swallowed
darkness of women

who know something more.

Wolf Endarkenment

I walked among an old man's death,
His wreckage of bent metal and shattered glass,
Torn trees strewn around him, roots flailing like sick
Octopuses, the scent of burnt plastic and torn earth.
A woman birthed a child in the debris and died.
The child survived endarkened
with wolf.

         i say wolf—
i mean a dark one semilunared
on my tongue   i speak wolf
and read language in leaves
whose green autumns
to death   the wolf who speaks me
carries my heart

A view of the art deco city
only strengthens the narrow vision.
A clicking keyboard sounded like contentment.
The turquoise woman raged
As her butterfly clipped
Hair escaped tongs, her indignation
A spray of brown and green like a sick fountain.
I could not be her keeper.
A clicking keyboard
    began to sound
        clipped.
Symmetrical architecture loomed in the sun
Over the wall of fear I built. It shattered
Every time the phone rang, until a wreckage

Of windshield wipers, jumper cables, newspapers,
And water bottles piled at my feet.
I couldn't afford lunch.
I couldn't afford not
        To run away

to wolf who shows me the enlightenment
to which i was chained
her fangs
puncture
its full spectrum until red rosin
    drips
        down
            granite
    a fall
of flesh
i would not speak her
if i did not break
and she would not speak me
we would not tenderly annunciate
each other's tongues
with our hearts

The Wolf in Her Dreams

When her husband becomes a wolf, she doesn't panic.
She's thought about this before,
becoming wolf, in her dreams.

He runs through the forest, dark, naked.
He falls into streams, he digs his fingers into mud.
When he comes back, he drips with water and blood.
His fingernails hold crescents of dirt.
Patches of wet fur glisten on his chest.
He has a wild-eye gleam.

And he lies to her at first.
He says he was reading—reading!
She knows this for untruth, but she keeps listening.

When he's rinsed the mud and the blood
from his skin, when he's peeled off the wolf pelt
and plucked fur from his heart and washed it away,
he's ready to tell—and she does not panic,
because she loves him.
Because she had already feared
a greater unknown.
And she's seen this before, in her dreams.

When she calls her best friend to tell her
        my husband, he's a wolf
she supports her.
When she calls her parents to tell them
        my husband, he's a wolf
they love her.

When he comes home because he loves her,
she's already discovered she is loved beyond words.

She reaches for him with her glistening paws—

A Ghazel for Wings

My lungs are a flock of ravens with black wings;
We creak in the ash, our crooked branches for wings.

Ravens call mind and memory their house of air,
sunlight, and clay—
I too am made of these sore wings.

When we exhale feathers
Through leaves, we implore wings.

We wolf what weeps the breath of blackthorn
That quivers the river of worn wings.

We circle   We circle   We circle
With the water   With the clay   With the web
Of what was   Of the unfolding   Of what will be
          sprouting from our mouths, forlorn wings.

Tongues feather and reach the root of the snake
Snatching from the nest of speckled unborn wings.

Rising in undulations, black crests of waves
Shimmer mountains of war's wings.

I toss the ash's seed into the kindled center
That wakes metaphor's wings:

                The sun, the sun!
                That blooms inspiration
                Black dressed dancers of breath

Drop your ash
Let go the breath
And sing to the morn's wings

Weave red rosin of life; coyotes and foxes
Swallow death into their shrines that restore wings.

A wind crossing three trees sings
The lost lore of wings.

Wolf Fragments II

shadows keep me company
we have tea in the afternoons
& red wine at night

we lap wind in
strokes a cat grooming
her furshadows
spell over we
clutch
for a sense of doom
which vellums shadow's tongue

Wolf, my edges blob.
Where do I begin
And you end?

Wolf Stories

Wolf—
We robe you in tyranny
You are not the good dogs
You're costumed forlorn

Wolf—
You were given teeth, you were given claws
You were given the moon for eyes
Let's feather you with fear
The night is wolf shaped

Who are you without—Who are we without—
Wolf within?
You will wolf us
Down into animals

Do we really wolf you? Is our wolf of the wolf ours?
Can we rend from you
Our ensemble of strung wolves?
Can we find wolf
Untrapped in our wolf?

But wolf snared us
In a trap

> Here lies wolf
> Written in a book
> Telling wolves

But I am wolf here!

Can we wolf
The wolf without story?
Let's follow wolf tracks and remember

Stories can wolf to you, wolf
We need not trap you in them
                              as wolf-
story builds on
                    Remember
                              our wolfkin
Emerges from old wolves

We don't need to pin
Our paws on our wolf
We can wolf our stories

                                        space
                              to breathe
                    in truth's branches of pine

My frame wolf be flawed

        but wolf   but you   but I:

                    we are not flawed

So let us wolf to story
Let us wolf to wolf

Skin Changers

After Noël Sturgeon

A call—
Can you hear
the moon's song

on thin branches at midnight?
The werewolf listens.

She can hear the moon
rising with her skin,
that liquid light an ecstatic

splash of electricity,
a crackle.

Werewolves, these people
whose skin changes, who sprout
fur and hurtle

through forests at *inter lupum et canem*—
the time between the dog and the wolf.

Creatures who listen
to their yearning,
a desire crooned by the moon's

increscence, who claw the land
like ocean waves at high tide,

persistent, overcome by a crash
of teeth & claws & tail. They rise
into winter nudity, they plunge into themselves.

The wolf enters the human
as the human enters the forest.

The scent of soaked earth,
of fur and licked bones, trails her
as she leaps over logs & roots & stones.

Here, absolutes cannot exist.
Here, children know.

We live in a gradient of gray,
humanimality unmasked
by feet planted in soil like sun-bent flowers,

by wings of windblown leaves,
by knotted faces found in twisted trees.

Something Green and Ancient

Blood and crushed yarrow,
something green and ancient.
I coax parsley from its grooved shell, the sprout
reluctant to crack open from its womb,
yet I cannot blame it as I cast
around for some sign of familiarity
in our corridors of concrete. The wind

in the wheat speaks my ancestors—
it whispers struggle and love;
the sun flashes on blood-
hardened blades swung for honor, for deep-
hearted rage.

When I begin from the ground
I stand on, the wind
in the corn tells me peacetime, bees
laden with pollen. And the wind
in the corn says spears divide
with murder; that only violence
quenches power's thirst. How is it we seek
peace by hastening death?

The raven laughs our folly as he slurps
from corpses. The sun
creeps into my dusk shade.
Wounds, packed with yarrow,
shudder, an open sting, my flesh
cracked, as a storm ready
to break across the dry desert; as rock
fracked by machines. When I listen to yarrow
tended by hands long turned into the flowers
they tended, what will I hear?

The wind rattles my bones
and clacks my teeth as I labor to love,
though I cannot relent what words
ancestors whisper to wolf in the wind.

Feathers

When September slips in the window
Like a forgotten lover,
Reaching for me from my burrow
                          With its hands of feathers

In the early morning croak of crows,
And I can smell
That someone has lit a fire,
                          An utterance of feathers,

Such that I can't remember if I'm seven,
In a log house my father built,
And he's kindled the first autumn fire,
                          Fanned the feathers,

Or I'm twenty-five in the wooded hollow alone
But for the cats, dogs, and calls of coyotes,
Having lit the fire myself
                          That spanned feathers,

But no, when you roll over
In a twist of sheets,
                          In a band of feathers,

And I hear a young tail thump softly on the floor,
A brief whine—When someone else's woodsmoke slips
Through the window
                          Like sanded feathers,

And I am here with you,
And we've struck our own match—
When you reach across
And slip your arm around my waist,

                    With the sustenance of feathers—

The Body Knows

You sprang from the womb
of a concrete floor, a cage
of iron that rattled your bones.

I saw you bite your tongue
with needle teeth that gleamed
white in dust dark
corners of those screaming cells.

Your silence held your truth,
your brown eyes glistened
fear as metallic red filled
your clenched tongue.

Red leaves fall around you now,
red as the blood that dripped
from your tongue, as trees sigh
into spindled winter. The impression

you leave on the ground grows.
I fear a sliver of you; perhaps you fear
some part of me, this crash
of interspecies. This chiasm of tongues

at the crossroads of imperfect speech.
Our bodies know truth:
a glance of teeth on skin,
raised hackles, softening eyes,
my clenched heart.

I Stole Your Sweater

I stole your green sweater. The soft moth-chewed one.
I know you know I stole it because you see me wear it.
I took your brown wool sweater,
the other moth-chewed one,

which I got blue paint on when we made Christmas
cards together. I gave that one back
because I thought maybe you were getting cold,

but I guess I'm not that worried
since I stole your sweater the color of goldenrod
flowers, or maybe mustard seeds, the one that opens
in the front and has brown buttons.

I returned your flannel pajamas, the ones you let me
wear the first night we spent together. But sometimes
I wear them when you're away, then press them back
into the drawer with your khakis.

I can't wear those khakis—I don't like khakis anyway.
I probably won't wear your t-shirts. I definitely won't
wear those button-ups with the collars.

Did you know we were agreeing to share everything,
even clothes, when we made those promises to each
other beneath apple trees veiled in summer?

The Morning You Didn't Make Coffee

Although we joke we should try something new for a
change and drink coffee, it's a lie because the only
time we've woken together

and not made coffee was your birthday party where I
left just before dawn, hours after

the other guests had gone, our first night together,
and that morning you asked me if you could make me

coffee as I stumbled in that unfamiliar dark where
I left your pajamas on your bed,
the green and blue plaid ones

I wear now when you're away and I'm home with the
cats,   but I didn't know you that well then, I declined
the coffee,

tired but brimming, already full, full like my cup now
with coffee that tastes like the morning you didn't
make any.

Wolf Fragments III

sup on wy/ord
            tablet etchings

    the dead alive
through blood written in stone
            carved

so that
the dark eats
my shadows feed

on bone   on clay   on stars

                        Wolf, you are more
            than two long strokes, two short strokes,
                with two meeting points in between
            a circle of which I can only make imperfectly
        a single long, vertical stroke like a dangling icicle
            a two stroked thing where they intersect at a
    crossroads, the vertical stroke long and hooked at the
    top like a shepherd's crook, the horizontal one, which
            is closer to the crook than the foot, short.

The House of Undoing

Wolf Fragments IV

the moon waxed and waned

twice

without our speaking

      the house
             empty
but for
      me
             two cats

   our many shadows

                 Wolf, are you consonant
                   Or are you vowel?

Edge of Wolf

You, fusillade of color—   Sing.
We die here
at the edge
where dog becomes wolf.

                        I gather acorns,
               cup them in my hands;
                  the world's seed,
                  fallen and brown.

Some need not boil
the acorn's poison,
they eat them raw and bare,
bare as the gray and gnarled oaks
in winter.   A love
      of some kind

                    falls,

    an acorn. Let me taste
                    your bitterness,
      your green unripened,
        before you   fall
                    and rot.

      The unfallen will not wither,
      will not cower
      beneath the sun's
        wrath who cracks
      a chasm between the clouds
    that suck back stars

into my mouth,
my stars of gathering.

That sword at his belt—
the unfallen will not perish
by its unblooded edge,
no—   they fly,
caught in a bird's black
beak, wolf's carrion
cousin, their color now
the edge of wolf
which I follow
as acorns roll
beneath my bare feet.

Acorn flesh autumns
and crumbles, a crunch
of bones and sweet rot
beneath mountains
in flame.

Loris

Once, even the sun could not tell
Where I began and where I ended,
For it rose like a slow loris
With two limp tongues
That cannot find the flower's deep nectar.
I haven't seen the moon
In days, her waning crescent
A dark hole. I've lost
The time and my feet wander
As I follow faint tracks:
Bird, squirrel, deer, cat.
Though the sun rises late,
It cannot account for my own
Late hour of rising—
Sucked dry, worm-eaten ear of corn,
The husk hiding the shape of my being, hiding me
Empty.
We finally fell into bed, humming our own songs
That merged into some sort of unity.

The Forest of My Undoing

When I free laurels and azaleas with my clippers,
wisteria-choked like prisoners,
I disturb moss ancient in its shape of ground.

When I clear last autumn's oak leaves
from the garlic bed, the brown blades twice as big
as my hands and soft from winter frost,
worms and grubs bedded beneath them writhe,
revealed, once content in their spring dark,
now homeless.

My rhythms of wake and sleep
no longer accompany the sun's,
the blue light of dusk my night.
Keening crows a cancer in my throat.
From the forest of my undoing,

wolf edges out of me,
ragged.

Blithe Flies

I hear the neighbors more now in their separation
and absence. Grass daggers in plumes,
open windows shudder into a dark desert.
Their new plastic swimming pool collects algae—
I can hear frogs congregate at its edge.

Before, I never caught the scuff of sneakers and boots,
the pad of four barefoot children running, but now
their unstepped echoes rattle in my head,
the unswung door so loud, the latch
that doesn't click. The porch corner gathers
clothes and a windblown pile of leaves.

My husband heard their explosive end as he sought
quiet among crickets at dusk—above the chorus rose
the wife's primal screams as the husband murmured
lake waves lapping to shore.

I clutch my husband's arm in the night,
my fingers digging into his anchored body,
alive but dying flesh—what if this, too, ends?

My summer sunflowers droop weary heads
at the yellow halo of their own fallen petals.
A heifer bellows as she lingers by her calf
whose darkened eyes
collect blithe flies.

Snared

A rabbit snared
and dangling
from a bent bough.
The body hosts all that is done to it.
It keeps
intruders who refuse to leave but don't
make themselves
at home. They don't fit.
They cannot be
forgotten.

They appear again
and again, here in the licorice of crushed tarragon,
here in ghosts left by hands
that hunted beneath denim and clasp,
here on the tongue
when salt mixes with liquor. Can't you hear them
rattling their bones—their hands quick
as the kestrel's wings.

The cold west wind ranges
from the mountain peaks
to the bare grove of birches. Bits of bark flap
as trees sway and creak.

Wolf Fragments V

when i don't know how to live
in this
defiled world this
despicable world so

                          i sever their hands

when earth gives as we take
and we take and
those men take

                        with their hands

here   this event

                  doesn't it mean

                     something?
                        Wolf, is the edge
                          Between us
                       Breath or break?

Goddess Sense

When a mare senses danger,
She alerts the herd.
Her ears prick
and her head rises from grazing.
She stops chewing and listens
With her whole body.
Her brown hide twitches, tingling—
She feels the danger.

Like when I walk down a street
And feel eyes that dagger my back,
Demeter smells Poseidon's desire.

The mare's warning ripples
Among the horses
Who raise their own heads,
Some snorting,
Not the contented huffs
Into my palm late at night,
But a terrible ripping sound,
The sound of fear.
Their eyes roll
White.

Do they run?
Demeter, do we flee?
Poseidon draws closer.

Blood-red poppies and barley grains
Scatter at our feet.

Demeter's hooves ring like requiem vespers
As the other horses clatter around me,
My herd, my kin, our manes and tails
Full sails that flood wounds wedged
Between despair and ecstasy. Our hooves
Pound through elk-sedge grass.

The Molester at the Mechanic

When I turned around to look,
because I had to,
to see who had entered
as I stood in the car mechanic's lobby
dimly lit like the entrance of a cave,
midmorning shortening shadows
drifting into corners interrupted
by flashes of sunlight on windshields outside,
when I turned around alone,
for my husband had stepped away
and the desk clerk had gone to fetch
my courtesy car, no one else but he
who entered and caused my shock witnessed it,
he whom I recognized merely
by his back-lit silhouette, further rounded now
with longer hair and unkempt beard,
and when he waved with his right hand as he entered,
a seemingly unthought gesture
before that hand fell to his side
and he uttered the word "Hello,"
a sound that rose like a bird taking flight
that dropped into the gathering blue,
shot by a bullet,
something incomplete,
and when I said nothing in response,
for my sight had scattered,
my hackles had risen,
thorns had sprouted,
when instead I turned carefully back to the empty
reception office like a prey animal slinking,

trying to keep hidden, but knowing
I have been seen, my skin tingling
warning signs of danger, ears pricked,
head and tail raised—I've alerted the herd,
we're ready to stampede—
and caught my breath, those years of yoga practice
had inched their way into my body after all,
though I still trembled
like the beginning tremors of an earthquake
while his silhouette loomed and stifled
the air that choked my lungs,
when my husband entered through a back door
and, outnumbered now, the intruder
slipped outside just as the clerk returned,
handed me the key to a Corolla,
which I think I thanked him for,
when already I had fled too,
had passed the man as he sat
in his red Volvo, unlooking,
when I walked by, unseeing,
with every inch of my flesh
looking, calculating, memorizing,
I realized
it wasn't him.

Yet I felt again
his predator's teeth.
They sank
into my withers.

Could I shake him off me?

Could I gallop away?

My Familiars

I wear your sweater as I walk by the garden
that has given us food and medicine,
the tomatoes and mint, the red bee balm;
I pass through dappled magnolia shadows that shade
thick moss; I follow our faint path to and from the
compost pile heaped with scraps, gritty remains of
morning coffee, weeds I've pulled.

These familiars hold me
and I hold them to myself like a letter,
pressed to the heart, that has just arrived from a far-
off lover who is traveling, or at war.
I hold them to fend off the dread
that I might see *him*.

As I step into
an unknown moment,
my familiars strengthen me:
the scratch of wool on my arms,
the garden with a scent of damp soil and minerals
where yarrow seeds blew and sprouted
their green, healing leaves.

You said you didn't see him
the last time I saw him,
and you're gone now, for a little while,
when I might see him again.

The man who thought by studying theory, he acted
truth, the man who unselved me,
who made my body unfamiliar to me by making it
his own
with hands that hunted,
like a man that plunders
a deer of her heart
but leaves the rest of her body
to rot.

The Weekend He's Away

I don't notice the first
morning. When I take the dog out to pee, when
I meditate, or let the cat jump through the front door

who ensures the morning, too, is rising, I don't
notice. I don't notice when I feed the animals, or fill
the tea kettle with tap water, flick its on button to boil.

My routine begins while he still sleeps, his body firmly
in bed, yet elsewhere, like a flower with its petals
that blossom toward the sun while its roots search

below earth's surface for water. Then as the sky begins
to blue and differentiate from the apple trees, he
enters the morning, too, a traveler who

needs a bowl of water to wash off the dust from
dreams. He clutches a mug of coffee over
a book as he opens like a morning glory. But today

he's not here to fill the morning, and like a
flower growing in a sidewalk cranny, I cast
about my day for water and deep soil, uncertain what

is missing, yet knowing it is he, his fingers that
untangle the knots in my hair, his frame that bends
around mine. Though I can name such a thing—yes,

it is he—I cannot say the absence as I cannot describe
texture of smoke that curls from an incense stick in
our bedroom, an ephemerality

I can only see and smell, but cannot feel with my skin.
I can speak of its ashy remains, its gritty soot that
smears on my fingers; I can tell of the herbal scent

that lingers, like the scent of blooms in an orchard,
and reminds me it wafted through the room, lightly
stained the painted walls an imperceptible gray.

I cannot speak
of how his absence feels, because it's only memory of
smoke.

Stone-Stepping

The wolf stone-steps with river-licked paws
Across the snarl of whirlpools.
She leads me through water that dizzies clouds;
She safeguards me past plunging water—
                              she, unrushed.

We search, her wet paws
Pointed North
And my heart clutched
In her teeth.
Or is that her heart I hold in my hands?

A hunger. A hunger twined
By wolf hearts,
Ghost tongues that speak the warp and woof
Of time woven in snow, bundled twigs
Of ash over dried pine.
I flick a match.
Light the pyre.

I step
Into death's remaking.
Shadows flicker the dark way.

Wolf Fragments VI

a bag full of severed hands

    in

        my memory   as if they
                                     were real

as if the hands

        were in
            my hands

      as if i (were i me)
          had severed them myself

to keep in
        a clear plastic bag

    for someone else to throw away   i couldn't

        i needed others to

          Wolf, what if our rended edges
               Were reversible
            Or could we mend them?

Wolf Fragments VII

teach me
> *earth's waters*
> *wash over we*
> *who stand beneath*
> *the moon your blood*
> *and our blood*
> *are one we*
> *scatter*

till the wolf speaks
> in stones
>> Wolf, are you something whisperable
>> Or unutterable?

Learning to Speak Horse

I.

When trees became road signs and lampposts
and paths paved roads;

when you were broken to the task
of sinew and bone clothed in dull hide,
your hooves cracked with dried blood;

when hard edges worked their angles,
body became shadow
        or no shadow at all—

the hard edges softened
into rose-gold.
Something else demanded.
Some other tongue said
               speak

II.

I am the color of a fallow field of corn,
My stalks shorn, my husks empty
and musting in the cold west wind.

The black dress that rippled
like ink spreading in water
I tore from my limbs.

The goldenrod wags clumps
of stagnant yellow at the field's edge.
I dig my feet in the cold soil.

Grey clouds loom, weaved
by women's hands that clutch
needles threaded by rain.

The wall of stone I sit on speaks
in a language slower
than I can understand.

III.

The humility I did not need as a child
I must lean on now as I return
to the first language of the earth.
Your soft lips winnow weeds for grass
    touch my hand
    my cheek.

The palomino tosses his cream mane,
hair I untangled knot by knot,
my fingers unthreading each strand.

Hedge Walking with Brigid

Does my strength wane as the sky waxes
in bitter release, the great white grain hard as a fist
that beats the ground like horses galloping?
Where is my craft now?

Does it seek the earth where those clenched fists
pummeled warm ground and dissolved to water?
We soften by earth's acceptance,
hardened hail to flowing water. Hubris to humility

is my threshold, here at earth's surface,
more known by my feet than my hands lost
in sky's folds of low-slung clouds.

Or does my craft come from the threshold itself,
the brink where air meets earth,
where fire flames toward the sky then returns
with snow that fills the hollow?

I am found where chaos converges
at the hedge.
How do I live as the ewe,
the hedgehog, the oak?

Spring Searches

Spring searches for me but finds only winter.
Violets seek the sun's lengthening light,

Caress my cheek; I do not know their newness.
Once, I didn't need to think of it,

I just felt; the animals told me.
Spring calls for me but I cannot answer

and it no longer recalls my heart's shape
that is shriveled and bent toward want.

It does not recognize my
twisted fingers taught

to fill an empty longing
with more longing.

It does not know my hands that
scrabble parched ground,

hands that seek to clutch
    this   and this   and

Who have you become? ask the nodding daffodils.
What is it that you seek and cannot find?

Their petals fade, spent from utter joy.

Nestling

Muscle-sore from gardening, at a park picnic table,
my husband and I watch water ripple light then dark
as fishing boats cut across the lake near our home.
The surface-green returns
in an impression of the shore. Canadian geese
call with spread wings as they honk goodbye
to their winter home, like when I blow my car horn
at the end of my parents' drive when I begin
my journey home. Maybe not goodbye,
but see you again soon.
A heron skims the green water, her blue
feathers a stormy sky at dusk,
she a river queen surveying her kingdom.

I'm thinking about the man we saw
in town wearing black suit pants and a visor,
his long grey hair braided down his back,
tapping a cane and shuffling across the square
in red plaid house slippers.
Our friend said, "The world is his bedroom."
As if a person could belong anywhere,
a town square, an alcove, a bench—
but if we belong anywhere,
where is home?
An urge tells me, go, search, yet another says to stop
and listen,
for how could I learn in a mere twelve years

the voices of the Blue Ridge Mountains
that thrust themselves before me
from our mother's body? I haven't yet heard
all the stories they lift to the sky. A mere two years
and I've only begun to hear the ancient oak
that stands guard over our home, whose branches
spread around me in a father's clasp.

You fill my cup with wine and together we drink
nectar from a far-away land
whose fruit ripened beneath the same sun setting
over this green lake. Your gift to me says
I am home with you, and I accept,
my head bowed.

Sister Mare
after Linda Kohanov

Horses

                rumble inside me

Horses

                beat in my chest

Horses

                with their flesh like love

Sister mare

    Let me weave your mane with daisies

    In return for your gift of milk to the wayfarer

Men and gods cannot catch us with their fetters

As my hands touch the soil, earth's dark grave

Sister mare

    Let me braid your tail with yarrow

    Your forelock with clover

Horses are the thunder in rain

A hammer to the thorn

Sister mare

    I'll make you a crown of forget-me-nots

    To ring around your blossoming ears

We rise in a moonlit sky, the palomino

Soft beneath my bare legs as she flings her seafoam

mane

Sister mare
    Teach me
    The way of the horse

Sister mare
    I yearn for humility
    Here in your gift of grace

I see you in the pool of my mind.
I am rounded at your feet.

In Between Dog, Crow, and Water

She makes bubbling sounds in the water
As she fishes for an acorn.
The splashes at the lake today come from above,
The world of air: a dog's sandy snout, her paws;
They pierce the surface. The lake accepts the soft
forms. It takes shape around them.

When fish leaped from below
Beneath the rising Hunter Moon, water rippled up
As scales crossed the liquid tympanum.

Neither fish nor dog remain
In the other's world.
They only visit for a while.

Though no fish break the surface as the rising sun
melts, the first frost that whitened the grass, the car
windshield, the wildflowers, their scent lingers.
A stench of sweet rot and wet sand.

I occur on the lake's shore, somewhere far
From the men with hungering eyes
Who thrust gas nozzles into plastic cans; I occur
Someplace in between
Dog, crow, and water.

Water shows me
How the world holds itself together,
The water like thick air,
Permeable, fluid, but cohered.

Water shows me
How blood runs through our veins.
Crows teach me
How to find speech without words.
The dog shows me
How to listen, how to walk
With dirt on my nose.

Language of Sand

Once, I was wind-
swept folly, searching
across the shore,
careless, crushing
scallop shells into fragments
beneath my feet.
The ocean took the shards
back into her body
to be re-formed
and now
I can no longer find them.
I must trust them
to the world.

Grasses along the shore were wind-
bent where god wrote to me in letters
of black sand.

Nights in a vacation house, the porch, my father
smoking a cigar, Neil Young on the stereo, and my
mother holding a book in her lap. We drink wine and
listen to the ocean
whose sound in the dark is closer
because you can't see it. It looms. Waves crash
through *Heart of Gold*'s harmonica. The moon clouds
our eyes.

Now I follow the shore
alone, barefoot,
My skirt heavy
from the dampened hem,
saltwater that pulls
and lulls me
as the ocean and I
listen to the moon.
No Hollywood lights,
no boardwalks, just dark mirroring dark
and sand.

the snake who speaks moon

she speaks to me
in fragments
her brown skin flashes
flecks of mica

    we startle   each other

I've revealed her winter home
beneath weeds I pulled
in damp mulch I shoveled

but she's quick
to slither beneath loose soil
as it warms in the spring sun

she and I are one
we live in mysteries
feared for loving
the dark where illumination
is chiasmic sunlight

she speaks to me in crescents
her flesh exclaims
the moon
like the tide
in its rise
and long recession

she gentles me as I read her speech

A Home I Could Never Call Lonely

Wind whipped
the tarp roof of the makeshift shelter. The sky
darkened. My husband, sitting
at a picnic table nearby and holding a book,
said, "I come here for the view."
The old man, crouched in tattered clothes beneath the
tarp, nodded agreement and patted his dog whose
bones jutted through taut flesh as he panted.

A week later, we sit behind books
stacked on the picnic table near remnants of the
shelter. He says he can't remember what
he was reading when he met the man
with the dog. But he flips the pages of a novel
by Coetzee, methodically,
pencil in hand. I wonder

if he thinks about the character Michael K.,
homeless, growing squash in the heat of South Africa,
as we sit near the shelter's remains
where a man that might be called homeless,

made his home.
A home I could never call lonely,
but rich with the solitude of stars,
stars that reflect on the lake
a million sparkling suns,
while I scurry away before dark
to the lamplit
comfort of my home.

Possessed

Three weeks with nothing but a suitcase—forgotten.
I've stuffed it back into the closet, on top of other
bags, sheets, and sweaters.
I shut the door to keep from seeing it all, as I ignore
the collection of tea mugs on my desk,
dust gathering on drawings, prints, and photographs
propped up and plastered on the wall,
as I avert my gaze from
the stack of papers, taxes, schoolwork,
letters, and cards.

> Lacewing larvae collect carcasses and vegetation
> by impaling the matter on spikes
> that protrude from their spines,
> saved leftovers from their lunches.

> I surround my desk with feathers and pinecones,
> seashells, rocks,
> seed packets, and dried flowers.

Satin bowerbirds keep anything blue they can find.
The males, whose feathers are a deep blue-purple,
line their nests with blue treasures, while the females
judge the suitability of the male's blue mirroring blue.

> My cats swagger
> across my desk, sidestepping my stacks of notebooks.
> They find their favorite places to sleep, in corners,
> on windowsills, the pillows on the bed.
> They follow patches of sun.

Bone-house wasps build their nests
with ant corpses.

I think of clothes in drawers, the closets, Tupperware
with no lids, lids with no bottoms, inkless pens,
stuffed animals, glass bottles, a cracked crystal ball,
candles, a map of Middle-earth where there are

The mad hatterpillar collects
shed pieces of its own body
on its head.

dragons. What can dragons do with their hordes
of gold, besides sit on gleaming swords, cups, and
crowns and breathe fire on some gold-sickened fellow
fool enough to try to thieve from the king of thieves?

Decorator crabs camouflage their shell
by affixing plants and creatures to themselves,
which they keep even as they grow
into a new shell.

My friend's house burned down this spring.
Nothing but charred and scattered pages remain.

I wonder if he catches himself remembering
his blackened hoard of
stolen pint glasses, dull swords,
and tarnished crowns.

Dragon-sick with loss.

Wolf Medicine

Let me give you my medicine, the wolf said,
As we stepped into the river flowing,
While stones sang runes in the riverbed.

She told long tales of wolf bloodshed,
Of Ghost Wolf and Snowdrift's bleeding,
So let me give you wolf medicine, she said.

They placed rewards on the outlaws' heads,
Men's revenge for livestock killing,
As stones sang runes in the riverbed.

Wolves died by men who reared warheads
For the aggrieved act of hungering.
You need wolf medicine, she said.

Gunshots fired and two dogs bayed
Through Montana's prairie flowering
While stones sang runes in the riverbed.

The wolf lifted her great white head,
The waters strongly flowing,
Then forlorn howled for what has been unsaid
While stones sang runes in the riverbed.

Shapeshifters

Wolf Fragments VIII

suppose my heart

once wolf eyes

carnations blood

until she sucks in shadows

of flowered solitude

or licks in place of craft—

          the dirt
the fucking dirt

               Wolf, I am only consonant
               Without your round howl

Transformation

When wolfsbane blooms
and the autumn moon is bright

the great wolf comes.

The wooded thicket follows with eyes of thorns
as she leaves behind clawed hearts
and splintered bones speckled with red blood.

When black branches and thorns tremble
song, the wolf says,

before Hecate grasps daggered purple aconite

and crickets sound the clotting dark

not a twig snaps
or a dried leaf cracks,

i smell air fear-hardened and lit by a perverse
midnight sun i could stamp out with my wretched
breath
the same fear that stained the tender fur of my young
stained and strangled them
blood and fear became them
metallic and honeyed rot

when willow's wings tremble

i know you by your signs

broken twigs rended earth
i hunger now
i see blood pulse blue beneath skin
press from bones it seeks
the way out seeks
blood trembling bones that set loose blood
doe's blood stag's blood
their children's blood found the way through them
their children like mine will not return

and i hunger

when leaves redden and freeze in plumes of blood

when the autumn moon is bright

i hunger to devour your greed

Let's talk specifics on sprouting fur

Have you ever been so ecstatic,
      you've ripped off your clothes,
      that necklace from your ex,
      or your high heel shoes
         and flung them
into the wind?
             or over

                    a cliff?

            What if you were a werewolf?

Have you ever wanted to howl
      with rage
      or delight?

             Might you be a werewolf?

If you stand naked
before a wolf, you become a wolf.

You can tell a werewolf is a werewolf by the
identifying wound:
      bruises, broken bones,
      split lips, a gunshot hole
      or malleus maleficarum burned into fur
      all of these in the shape
      of the Inquisitor's absolute.

Have you ever stood naked
      before a mirror and seen
      a wolf instead?
            You could be a werewolf

Maybe you keep a werewolf garden:
    wolf's milk: orange slime
    wolf's fist: white mushrooms
    wolf's claw: club moss
    wolf's bane: poison in a purple flower

Or you might wear lipstick the blood of roses,
    or you eat poppies and swoon naked
    on a friend's rug patterned with tangled ivy.

Have you ever wanted to devour
    your dinner?
            or slurp sunshine?
            People might think you're a werewolf

Have you ever wanted to love?
    and love
            and
                    love

                            a werewolf?

Have you ever been told you're too irrational?
    or too sensitive?

Have you ever been a woman?
If you dehisced
the cage around your heart,
you might find
it's stuffed
with fur.

only the summer sun

i am a bear,
berserk blind and crashing,
i wield bone-teeth and claws
to defend my young, my den.

must i worship only
the summer sun?

i crave raking claws
of winter, the desert of snow
fierce around me
as i curl and i curl
in the dark.

paw follows paw—
my nose stories
the cave's windshapes—rabbit fur,
fox scat, berry flower—my ears
tingle at rustle
of toad and leaf. let me hold
so still
moss creeps up my spine.

wing follows wind
but my ears do not hear
bird song, nor can i taste
my tongue for my tongue
cannot utter
the unwhisperable. inside me,

a mountain looms
as it grows bones
and teeth of the once
living; they begin to clack.
a hunched woman in bear fur
stands over a bone-marked grave
where she gathers nettles,
her calloused fingers heedless of their sting.

This is not me

It is the poem
Which grasps for affinity
With the world
I see unfinished,
Remaking, renewing,
Hungering,
Like two crows
Who tirelessly
Leave and return,
Seeds clasped
In their black beaks
To fill the bellies
Of their blind young,
All wet feathers
And mouths
And hunger,
Yet to grow wings for flight.
In my unfinished
Making
I always believe
I've arrived at the end,
That I've found
The answer at last,
Only to be teased
By the tulip poplar who keeps
Planting seeds and branching leaves.
I arrive

At the beginning
Of something else,
Some new piece of me
That has only begun
To emerge.
Even death
Holds the beginning as worms,
Who eat my flesh,
Are eaten by birds
Who lift their wings
To the sky and I
Become wings
I become
Air

A Vegetarian Tries to Eat Rouget:
A Greek Chorus

Our heroine sits near the sea,
The salty air so thick she could swallow it like
molasses.
The Fresh Caught menu announces itself
On others' plates of fresh seafood,
And those eating from the flesh
Tremble and exclaim in delight:
The fish tastes just like the sea!
She gazes, allured
And sickened.

> I am like a horse in winter
> Who has caught the whiff of spring grass:
> I'm at the beach!
> Shouldn't I eat fish?

O, Mnemosyne, goddess of memory—
How long has she not eaten meat?
But like the last cigarette she didn't smoke
But tossed in the trash, victoriously,
The years had slipped by without thought.

> When was the last time
> I ate fish?
> Do you remember?

Her lover, oh most beautiful husband of hers,
Of the crepuscule light and libraries,
Recalls just a week ago how delicious
His Parisian oysters on the half shell
Smothered in lemon juice tasted.

Oh, and remember that time I ate
Oysters in Los Angeles?
Each ocean has its own
               Subtle
               Flavor...

She watches the pearly waves
Of the wine-dark sea
Crash to shore. Would the rouget
Taste just like the ocean?
Water beads on her glass of Santorini.
The golden liquid drips from the rim,
Racing the drops of sweat that slither between her
breasts, falling, falling.

               Can you truly be at the sea
               If you don't taste its fruits?
               Can you experience a place
               If you don't eat their food?
               I'm only asking because
               I'm teaching logic next semester.

Oh, what pressure! Oh, Athena of the wise decisions!
See how she swoons? Our heroine has lost her way!
Help her!
She falls
Prey.

               Forget it—just this once.
                    I'll take the rouget.
               She will taste just like the sea.
                    She is   already dead
                                   After all.

The server plunks a plate on the table
That tips on the ancient cobblestones.

A red, herb-smeared fish stares up at her,
A vacant Mona Lisa with a secret,
A sliced grapefruit bearing tender red beads
Of juice, a tail, and tiny fins.
A blood orange
With eyeballs.

She gulps her warming wine, unable
To peel her eyes from the rouget's
Dead ones.
Oh Theia, what sight you reveal!

I shouldn't waste the dead now.

She fumbles out the napkin-wrapped silverware,
The mantras of should's and ill-conceived
Apollonian logic souring her tongue,
Then forks the fish's fillet which flakes apart
And gapes
Like its dead-open mouth.
She looks up at her husband who has a fish gyro
Half-way drawn to his lips.

I don't know if I can...

She returns her fork to the plate.
She can't eat the rouget like her husband
Tossed back Parisian raw oysters,
Or like Les Claypool's El Sobrante Fortnight man
Who slurps the world down like a Tabasco slathered
clam—

I wasn't expecting
Eyeballs.

then   somewhere

in the blue deep

Oh, Amphitrite! Oh, Salacia!

i slip from a net

Of the calm and salty seas

i wriggle my fins and tail

With the crab's claw on your forehead!

free

of   expectations

We Invited Jean Genet
and Woody Allen for a Drink

But what we said about them I can't remember.
You and I both agreed relationships form

out of who one believes the other is, projection,
something Stendahl called seeing a leafless wintry
bough as a galaxy of scintillating diamonds, a crystal
encrusted twig.

Although we can't call this our first date because we
didn't know then what we know now, as we emptied
glasses of beer into our mouths, and the glasses long
stood with foam residue

Drying on the rims, we saw some version of ourselves
like we see just a fraction of the moon at a time.
While the weeknight called others to their homes,

we filled each other with our lives,

and when we parted,
something like a phantom
went from me into you,

and it went from you
into me; it entered us
silently, a seed

of desire, self of the self, self
of the other, other of the other,
a seed that held

the other parts of the moon's phases,
its waxing and waning, its eclipses by earth's
shadow such that even the self is hidden

from the self, a seed that held a motion slower
than the moon's phase change, a seed
that narrated

you and me

and when we parted, we were as changed
as when you walk into a cinema in daylight
and stumble out two hours later in the dark

the self forgotten and holding
another's story.

Snakes Kin

venom fuels our veins
and drips from our fangs
your trigger a massacre
on sun-basked flesh
we writhe
on the ground branded
a sin sinner betrayer of man
you scream that
we've made you

sin

                              sweat
beads on your
                              face enraged
flames red
you bury your hate
beneath our mounds
of earth and expect us
to keep it
you touch our darkness
like chemicals
poison wells
while you say
we are evil
and you demand
that we repent
                              our meadows
freeze
                              your hate

flames through
our teeth
                needle
out of the earth refused
like a wounded fetus
in an unwelcome womb
of honeyed mare's
                milk flows
from our forked
                tongues
find truth find
the poison you slipped
into our drink
we speak your hate
into fire
it walks like smoke

Sorrow Flowers

I picked from your garden of sorrow flowers;
Chrysanthemums and daisies count the hours.
Yet, fetid brown, their lure disguised your powers.
Veiled artifice, thorned roses loomed like towers.

You hid your heart, your soul already scoured.
These phlox, once purple, rotted black to fear
By ivy's furry fingers that devour.
Your soured nettles, poison brewed, I clear!

I banish! Wolf bares her fangs that deflower
What silence speaks: your bitter fruit.
By tooth and claw, she pins your truth
And rends soiled vines long gone sour.

Each coil unsnarled, each step away, from wolf's
Rich soil, faint snowdrops bloom my rebirth.

The Book of Unfixed Stars

Untangle your mane and tail with my fingers.
Pluck out the barbed burrs of autumn,
Dried seeds like Spiny Star Astrea snails,
Gathered in your hair from miles of forest trails
We'd navigated that day. Pick out stones

In your hooves wedged from rivers
We followed only for a time but then would chart
Our own way while the river rushed onward
To join with other, distant waters.
Curry your thickening coat until its black shines

The brightness of snow in a clear night sky.
Stuff your feeder with alfalfa and timothy.
Fill your bucket with icy water that shimmers
A thin edge between this world
Where I have found myself in relation to you,

And the springs of another. Knowing,
But unable to endure, drowning
In knowing that this would be one of our last,
That soon we will be lost,
I linger before you to say goodnight

And brace my feet as you rub your forehead
Against my chest, as you press me with your white
Star that glows like a creature's unwavering eye
In the night, white brilliance

89

In your sea of black,

And for a moment
Pegasus,

                No longer hobbled in the sky,
Reaches down
And grazes me with his wings.

Wolf Floods the River

The moon eclipses my sight as she arches
across my breast, cracks open ridged mountain of
bones. She rakes me with fibrous tendrils of dusk.

Raven!
Lift your wings.
The light is flesh-
thick beneath us.

Each one of them who hungered with their eyes,
reached for me with vile fingers, live in me as
poltergeists
who rattle
the windows
shatter
the glass
and set fire—

> *We are still here* they say
> *With our hands of hemlock*

I still remember.
I've dampened smoldering remains of flames
but ignored the explosions above me.

Wolf floods the unpoisoned river along my ridge of
bones, we swim deep, deep into the water,
my fingers for sight—
her fur,
her tongue.

Now—
I devour
their vile fingers.

Beneath white rapids
my white teeth turning
to the moon.

Magic Speaks Aloud

Once upon a wolf

when I stripped red
robes and rules

laws became growth
            and fall of leaves

my alphabet
no longer cowered
beneath the bed

but howled
a full lettered meadow

Wolf Fragments IX

Wolf,

i transform

with you but without

you   my voice

my own

as the night

          mare rises from the urned ashes
of word

          wounds

Chapel of Wolf

Like the man on the Sistine Chapel ceiling
who reclines to both receive god and touch god,
I lie back, humble and afraid. The wolf
who jumped through the window, who broke in
with her two cubs, she who I feared, stands over me.
Our bodies mirror each other.

Touching wolf, receiving wolf; that magical mundane.
Angelic earth. I gather my craft in a basket of woven
words. Catch the comfrey blooming and the bones
casting. It's not just two single points that unite like
two fingers. Our whole bodies meet. And she says, you
do not have to fear me.

Like I am her cub, she presses her snow-damp fur to
mine; She knows one day I will be my own
but first I must learn to speak the language of leaf,
root, and river. With her whole body she speaks,
with mine I listen. The wind stirs and returns the cold
of winter, voices hold the crackle of ice.
A cold wind comes. Winter has not succumbed
so easily to insipid summer after all. She holds,
she holds. She spreads on the yellow lips of daffodils.
The chapel of wolf huddles beneath frosted pine,
frozen branches. Huddles and thrusts
like a mountain heavy with the weight of ice.

Receive to touch. Stretch down to touch. The point
where we meet thickens to slush, like the air that
trembles around a scop

        chanting
        incantations
        against
        the three
The place where mystery opens like a cave,
where words are carved into air.

Spirit rends the threshold,
rips a tear in invisible flesh—
                red, white, running, blue,
                yellow, green, black,
                blue, brown, purple, warm
colors enter the air like a specter.

What is this mystery from the dark?
The people, they had heard,
they went about, milling and mumbling with
incoherent speech, their voices muffled.
Their foreboding urge—

        go
        see the thing
        in the woods
        in the dark woods

What is this mystery from the dark?
From the sundered
 Earth? An entity of colors,

Woman.

ACKNOWLEDGMENTS

Thanks to the editors of the following publications for curating the following poems, some of which appeared in different versions:

"This is not me" in *Tiny Seed Journal*
"Light Eaters" in *Wingless Dreamer*
"Learning to Speak Horse" in *Kakalak Anthology 2023*
"Donning Freya's Cloak of Feathers"
in *Eternal Haunted Summer*
"Sister Mare" in *Heartwood Literary Magazine*

Boundless gratitude to my teachers who've nurtured my love for reading and writing, especially Laura Hope-Gill, who shared with me dogs and magic; Dale Bailey and your careful attention as I revised *Wolfcraft*; and Greg Jenkins, for suggesting to me twenty years ago I major in English which has haunted me since. And to my classmates, particularly Susan, Ralph, Valerie, and Carol, for their companionship as we persevered through the alchemy of school. Thanks to Poetry Hickory open mic attendees for listening to drafts of my poems, to Taste Full Beans for supporting a poetic community, and to Lenoir-Rhyne University Fine Arts and Communications department for their support and love for the written word.

Thank you to my publisher Broken Tribe Press for the 2024 MFA Graduate Award and your assistance as I learn to navigate the publication process.

And I must acknowledge Wardruna, whose rhythms can be found in much of *Wolfcraft* (I recommend you listen to their music as you read).

I am indebted to Jaki Shelton Green and Scott Owens for reading and offering kind words to put on the back of this book; and Matt Avery for the beautiful cover.

Thanks to Lauren, my first reader of many of these poems, and to Emily, for friendship, hikes, and evenings with Monty Python and the Holy Grail; and all the Woods, my NC family. Thanks to my faery godmother, Michelle.

Thanks to my mother, for being my first teacher, for teaching me a love for books, and for reading everything I've written. Thanks to my father, who taught me how to love and attend to our natural world. A deep thanks to my husband who has nurtured and inspired my creative life from our beginning. And I can't leave out our pets, who will read this acknowledgment in their own ways.

And to the wolf, for dreams and visions.

ABOUT THE AUTHOR

Narya Rose Deckard, winner of the Broken Tribe Press MFA Graduate Award, is an Appalachian writer with poems curated in journals such as *Tiny Seed Press, The Dead Mule School, Eternal Haunted Summer*, and *Kakalak Anthology*. She earned her BA from UNC Asheville and her MFA from Lenoir-Rhyne University's Thomas Wolfe Center for Narrative. She lives in Valdese, NC with her husband, cats, dog, and chickens and teaches writing at Lenoir-Rhyne University. *Wolfcraft* is her first book of poems.